COLLINS PICTURE DICTIONARY

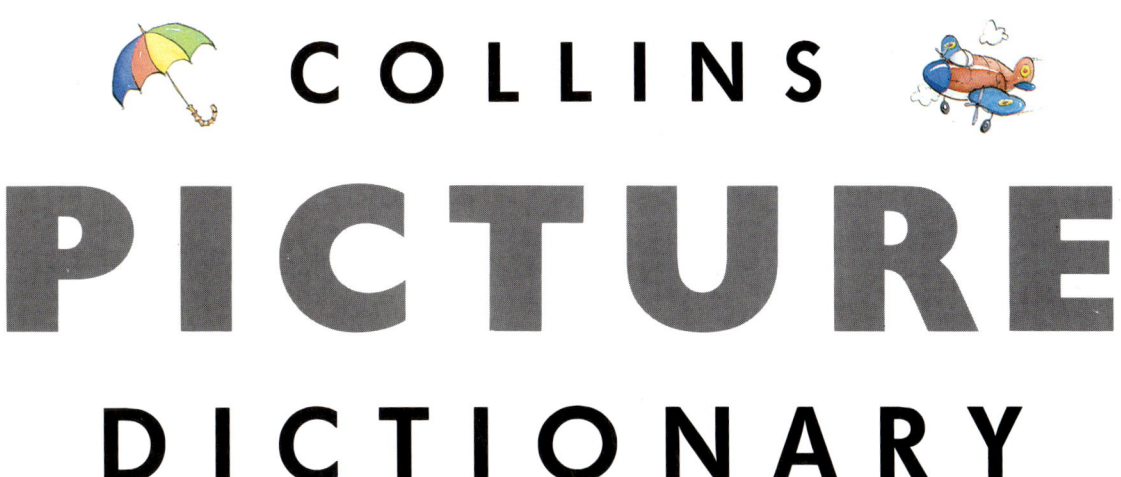

Written by
Dianne Lane and Elizabeth Peel

Illustrated by
Andy Cooke

COLLINS

Contents

- 3 Introduction
- 4 Me and my family
- 6 My body
- 8 My house
- 10 In the kitchen
- 12 In the garden
- 14 At school
- 16 Going shopping
- 18 At the café and restaurant
- 20 Going to the park
- 22 Sport
- 24 Doctors and dentists
- 26 People and jobs
- 28 Town and city
- 30 On the farm
- 32 At the seaside
- 34 A port
- 36 An airport
- 38 At the station
- 40 In the car
- 42 Space and space travel
- 44 Machines we use
- 46 Measuring things
- 48 Words for stories
- 50 Time
- 52 Colours and numbers
- 54 Opposites
- 56 Action words
- 58 Position words
- 59 Words in this book

William Collins Sons & Co Ltd
London · Glasgow · Sydney · Auckland
Toronto · Johannesburg

First published in Great Britain 1989 © William Collins Sons & Co Ltd

All rights reserved. No part of this publication may be reproduced, stored in a retrieval system, or transmitted, in any form or by any means, electronic, mechanical, photocopying or otherwise, without the permission of William Collins Sons & Co Ltd, 8 Grafton Street, LONDON W1X 3LA

ISBN 0 00 190054-4 HB

Typeset by TDR Photoset, Dartford
Printed and bound in Spain by
Grupo Nerecan - Tonsa, San Sebastian

Introduction

Here is a first dictionary for young readers. It contains over a thousand words, arranged by topic and illustrated with clear, lively pictures.

The book may be used on many levels. Children can begin by identifying the pictures and accompanying words. As their reading improves they can tackle the definitions which are written in clear, simple sentences and listed alphabetically within each topic. This means children will develop early dictionary skills, which may be extended by encouraging the use of the complete alphabetical list on pages 59-64. Here every word introduced in the book can be found with its page number.

Some less familiar words have been included and it is hoped that adults sharing this book will take pleasure in extending and enriching children's vocabulary.

Me and my family

name Katie
surname King
address 5 Palace Street
Queenstown
age 6 years
birthday 7th June

adult This is another word for a grown-up.

auntie Your auntie is your mother's or father's sister, or the wife of your uncle.

cousin Your cousin is your auntie's or your uncle's child.

family Family usually means your mother, father, sisters and brothers.

friend A friend is someone you know well and like.

grandparents Grandparents are your mother's mother and father, or your father's mother and father.

- grandparents
- neighbours
- husband
- friend
- father
- parents
- wife
- brother
- twins

husband When two people get married the man is called a husband.

neighbours Neighbours are the people who live near to you.

parents Parents are your mother and father.

relative A relative is anyone who belongs to your family.

surname Your surname is the last part of your name which you share with other people in your family.

teenager A teenager is someone aged between thirteen and nineteen, who is not a child but is not completely grown up.

twins Twins are brothers or sisters born on exactly the same day.

uncle Your uncle is your mother's or father's brother, or the husband of your auntie.

wife When two people get married the woman is called a wife.

My body

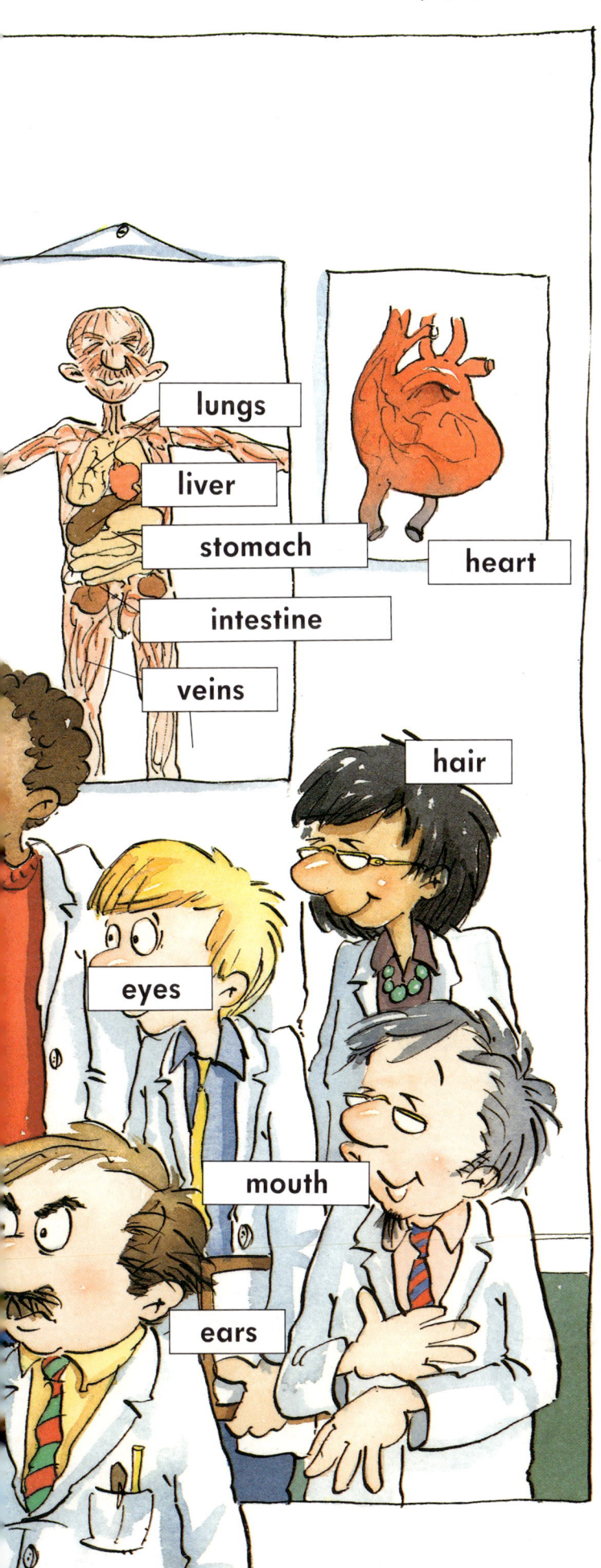

bones Bones are the hard parts you can feel inside your body. They are joined together to make your skeleton.

blood Blood is a thick red liquid which flows around your body. There are important things in blood to keep you alive.

brain Your brain is inside your head. You use it to think and to give instructions to the rest of your body.

heart Your heart beats and sends blood round your body.

intestine Your food goes down your intestine. It is a very long tube attached to your stomach.

liver Your liver is a large part inside your body. It makes things your body needs and helps to clean the blood.

lungs Lungs are like two sponges inside your chest. They fill with air when you breathe.

muscles A muscle joins two bones and helps them move.

ribs Ribs are the curved bones going from your back to your chest. You have twelve ribs on each side of your body.

skull Your skull is the bony part of your head.

stomach Your food goes to your stomach before it goes to your intestine.

veins Veins are like tubes inside your body. Your blood goes through them.

7

My house

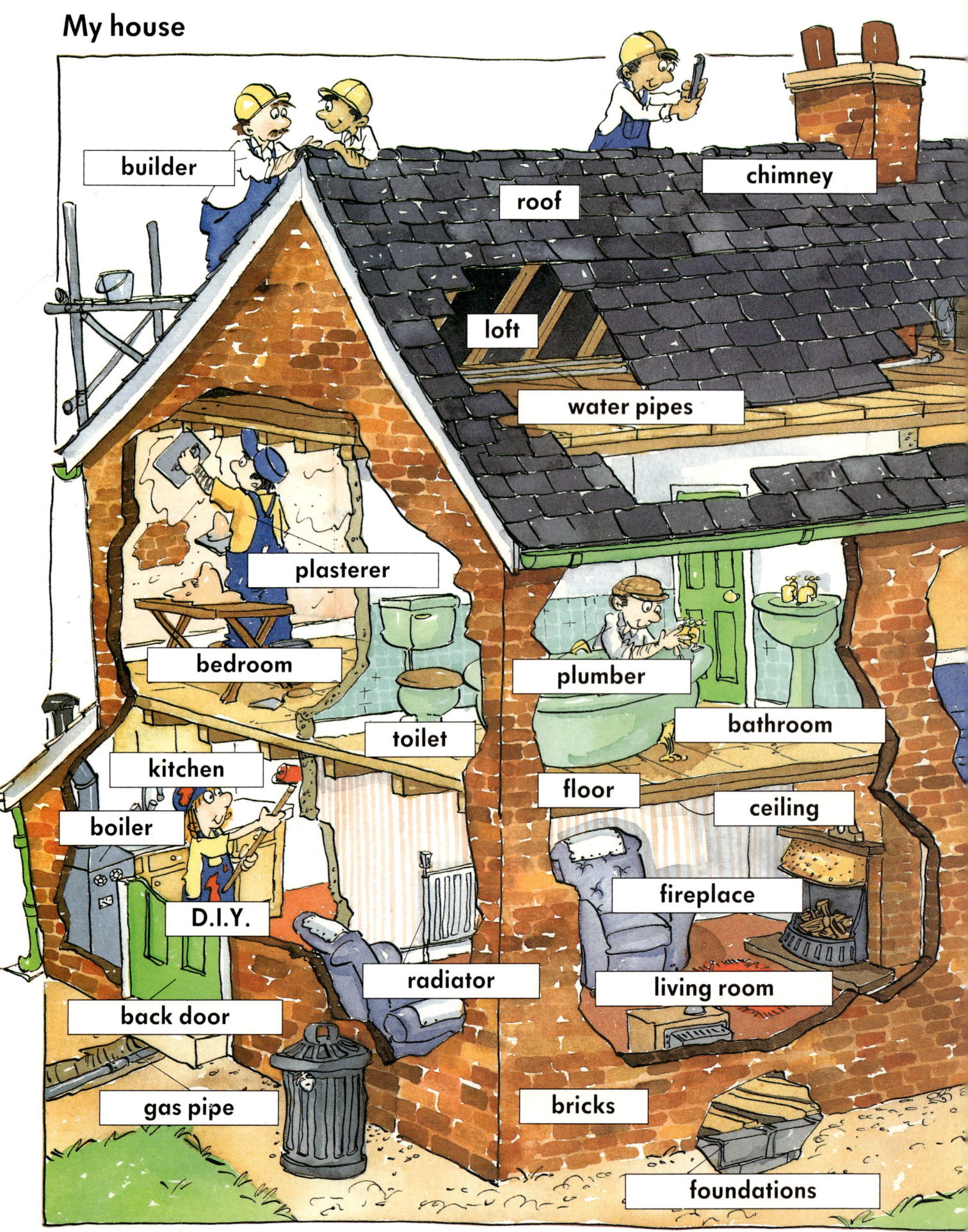

boiler The boiler makes hot water for the taps and the radiators.

D.I.Y. This is short for do-it-yourself. It means building or mending things yourself instead of paying someone else to do it.

electrician An electrician is someone who puts electric cables into buildings and mends them when they go wrong.

foundations The foundations are the bricks or concrete underneath a house. The foundations are built first so the walls have something strong and firm to stand on.

gutter When it rains the gutter catches the water from the roof and sends it down the drainpipe.

joiner A joiner is someone who makes window frames and doors out of wood.

loft The loft is the space inside the roof of a house. People often keep things in the loft.

plasterer This is someone who knows how to cover the walls and ceilings with plaster. Plaster makes the walls smooth and hard so they can be decorated.

plumber A plumber's job is to join water pipes to the bath, sink and toilet and to mend them if they leak.

radiator A radiator is filled with hot water to keep the room warm.

water tank The water tank stores the cold water for the house.

In the kitchen

crockery Crockery is a word for plates, cups, saucers and bowls.

dishwasher A dishwasher is a machine for washing and drying the dishes.

food mixer This is a machine that can mix or beat food very quickly.

freezer A freezer is a very cold fridge. It will keep food frozen for a long time.

grill A grill is used to cook food under a strong heat.

ingredients The ingredients are all the different foods you need to cook something.

microwave A microwave is a special oven that can cook food very quickly.

recipe A recipe is a list of instructions for making something to eat.

sieve A sieve has lots of tiny little holes. Flour can be pushed through to get rid of any lumps.

spatula A spatula is used for lifting and turning food in a pan.

steam When water boils, it turns into a hot mist called steam.

timer The timer rings to let you know when something has finished cooking. It can also be used to make the oven turn on or off by itself.

In the garden

berries Some plants have small round fruits called berries. The seeds of the plant are in the berries.

bud A young flower or leaf just starting to grow is called a bud.

bulb The root of some plants is shaped like an onion, and called a bulb. Daffodils and crocuses grow from bulbs.

bush A bush is like a small tree. It has lots of thick stems instead of a trunk.

compost Compost can be made from old leaves and plants. It is put on the soil and helps plants to grow.

germinate When a seed germinates it starts to grow and shoots appear.

greenhouse A greenhouse is a building made of glass. It is used to grow plants which need to be kept warm and sheltered.

moss Moss is a tiny green plant. It often grows in a lawn.

roots The parts of a plant growing under the ground are the roots.

seeds Seeds are made by plants. If they are planted they grow into new plants.

sprinkler This is a machine for watering grass or plants. It sprays water all over them.

weed A wild plant growing in a garden is called a weed.

At school

collage A collage is a picture made by sticking bits of cloth, card and paper together.

concentrate When you concentrate you think hard about what you are doing.

daydream You daydream when you think about nice things you would like to happen.

fidget When you fidget you wriggle about. Sometimes you fidget when you are bored.

measure To measure something means to find out how long or wide it is.

model A model is a small copy of something, such as a train or bridge. Models are often built out of cardboard.

register The register is a book with a list of all the pupils in the class. The teacher marks it every day to show who is in school.

weigh You weigh something to find out how heavy it is. Machines used for weighing are called scales.

Going shopping

aisle The aisle is the gap where you walk between the rows of shelves.

assistant A shop assistant helps you when you want to buy something and takes your money.

bargain A bargain is something that is being sold at a cheaper price than usual.

checkout The checkout is the place in a supermarket where you go to pay.

cheque You use a cheque instead of money to pay for things. When you write a cheque your money is sent from the bank to the shop.

customer A customer is someone who goes into a shop to buy something.

conveyor belt A conveyor belt is the moving strip of rubber you put your shopping on at the till.

credit card A credit card is a special piece of plastic you can use instead of money. You are sent a bill later.

department store This is a very big shop with lots of floors. It sells many different things.

receipt A receipt is a piece of paper the shop assistant gives you to show you have paid for something.

sale A sale is a special time when shops sell things at a cheaper price.

17

At the café and restaurant

chef A chef is a person who cooks food in a restaurant.

cutlery Cutlery is a word for knives, forks and spoons.

dessert Dessert is another word for pudding.

menu A menu is a list of all the food you can eat in a restaurant or café.

restaurant A restaurant is a place where you can buy meals. In a restaurant you are usually served by a waiter or waitress.

savoury Savoury is the opposite of sweet. Meat and vegetables are savoury foods.

self-service In a self-service café you help yourself to food from a counter.

snack A snack is a small meal you can eat quickly.

starter This is food you eat at the beginning of a meal. Soup is often a starter.

waiter/waitress A waiter or waitress is a person who works in a restaurant and serves people with food and drink.

19

Going to the park

acorn The nut from an oak tree is called an acorn.

conker A conker is the seed of the horse chestnut tree. It looks like a big shiny brown nut.

deciduous A deciduous tree loses its leaves every year in autumn.

evergreen An evergreen tree has green leaves all year round.

park-keeper The park-keeper looks after the park and keeps it tidy.

picnic A picnic is a meal you take with you to eat outside.

reeds Reeds grow at the edges of rivers and ponds. They are plants with tall, strong stems.

somersault When you do a somersault, you put your head down and roll your body right over it. Sometimes it is called a head-over-heels.

statue A statue is a large model of a person, often found in parks.

Sport

club When you play golf you use a club to hit the ball. A club is a long, thin stick with a curved end, made of wood or metal.

court Games like tennis and squash are played on a court. The ball must not bounce outside the lines marked on the court.

goal In soccer when a player kicks the ball into the net, he has scored a goal.

jockey A jockey is someone who rides a horse in a horse race.

pitch A pitch is a piece of ground marked out for playing sports like soccer or baseball.

racquet This is a special kind of bat for playing tennis or squash. It has an oval shaped head, with strings going down and across.

referee A referee makes sure players do not break the rules of the game.

score In most sports you keep a score to show who is winning.

umpire In some sports, like tennis, the referee is called the umpire. The umpire keeps the score and makes sure the players do not break the rules.

Doctors and dentists

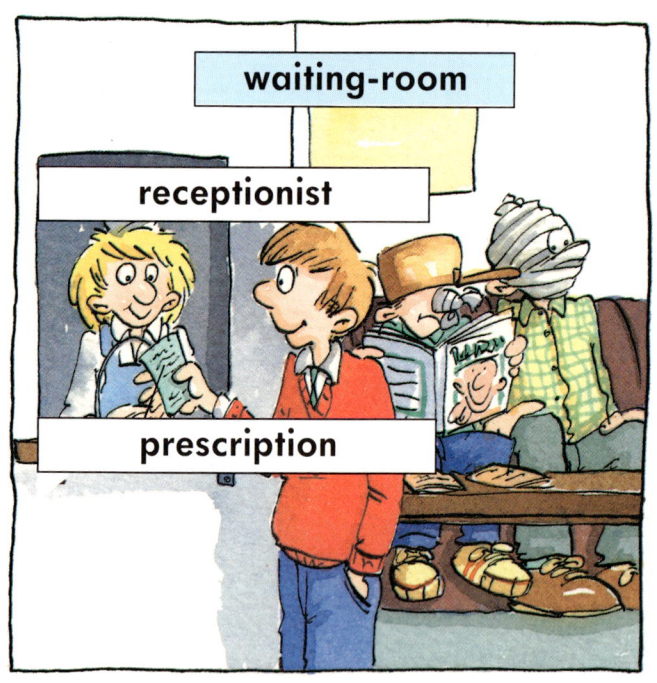
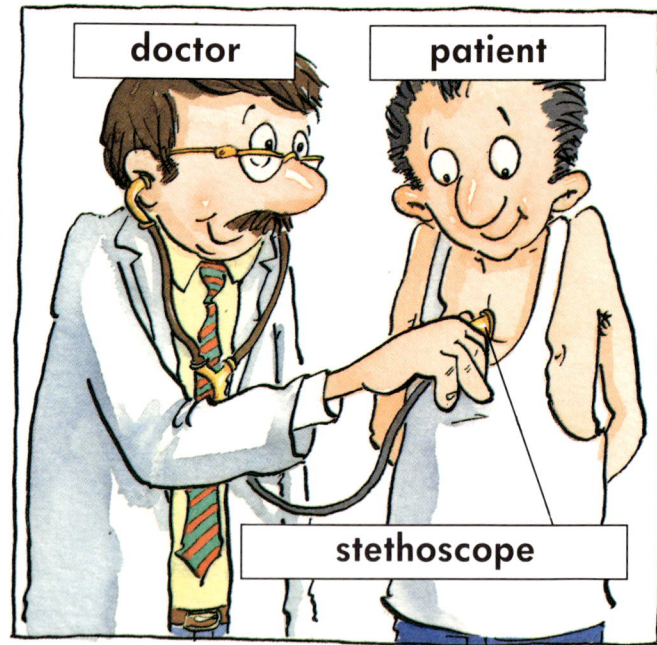
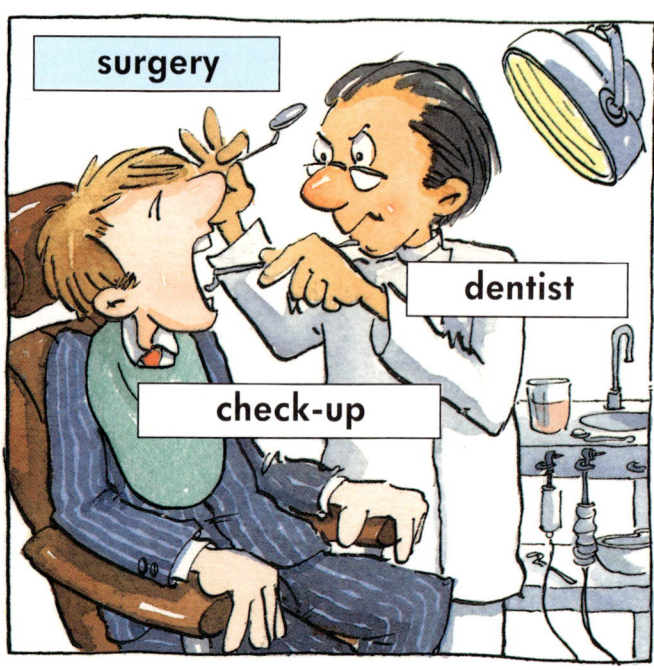
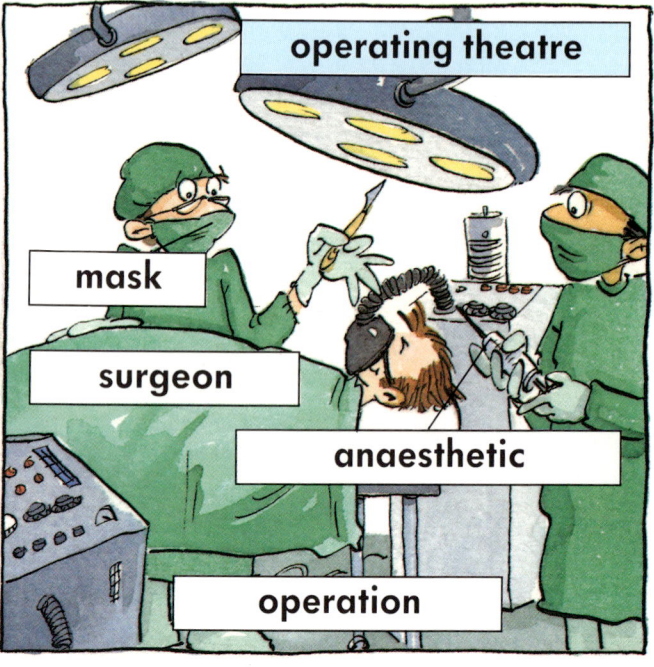

anaesthetic An anaesthetic stops you feeling any pain when you have an operation or a tooth taken out.

operating theatre This is a special room in a hospital where people go to have operations.

operation When you have an operation, the surgeon looks inside your body and makes it better.

patient A patient is someone who is ill and is seen by a doctor.

prescription This is a piece of paper the doctor uses to write down any medicines you need from the chemist.

receptionist The receptionist is the person at the doctor's or dentist's who arranges the times for people to come.

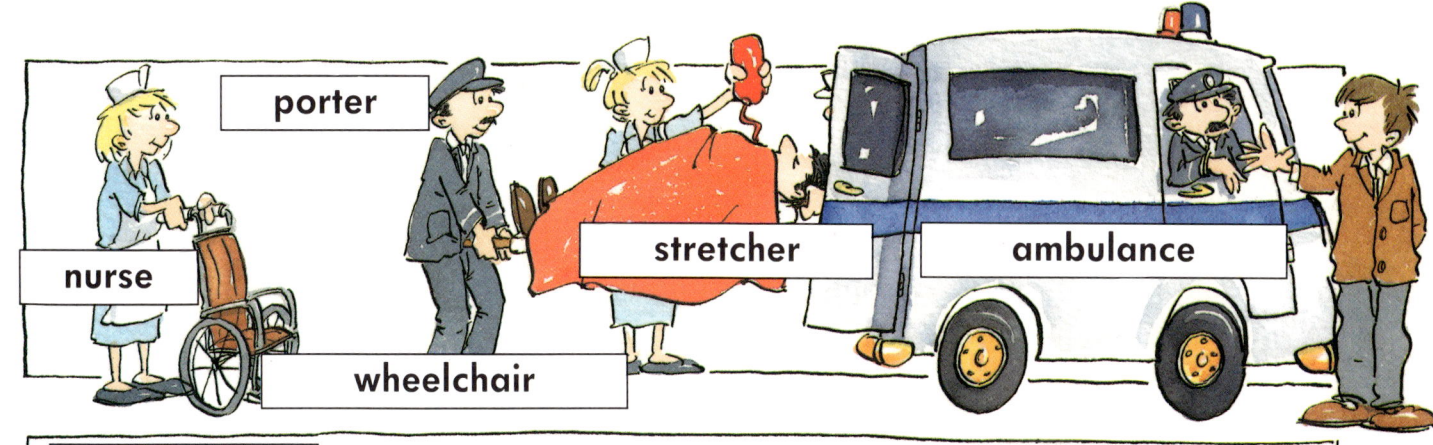

stethoscope The doctor uses a stethoscope to listen to your heart and other sounds inside your body.

surgeon A surgeon is a doctor who does operations.

surgery This is the room where you see the doctor or dentist.

syringe A syringe is a small plastic tube with a needle at one end. It is used to give people injections.

thermometer A thermometer measures the heat of your body. This is called your temperature.

ward In a hospital, the big rooms where the patients sleep and rest are called wards.

People and jobs

accountant An accountant gives people advice about their money.

architect An architect draws and plans buildings and makes sure they are properly built.

computer programmer A computer programmer writes lists of instructions, called programs, for computers to use.

engineer There are many different kinds of engineers. They draw and plan machines, bridges or roads.

journalist A journalist works for a newspaper or magazine, and writes about important things that happen.

judge A judge works in a court and decides how people should be punished when they have done something wrong.

mechanic This is someone who mends cars or other machines.

politician A politician is chosen by people to help make laws and run the country.

scientist A scientist is someone who does experiments and tries to find out more about the world around us.

secretary A secretary works in an office, answering the telephone and typing letters.

vet A vet is a person who looks after animals when they are sick.

27

Town and City

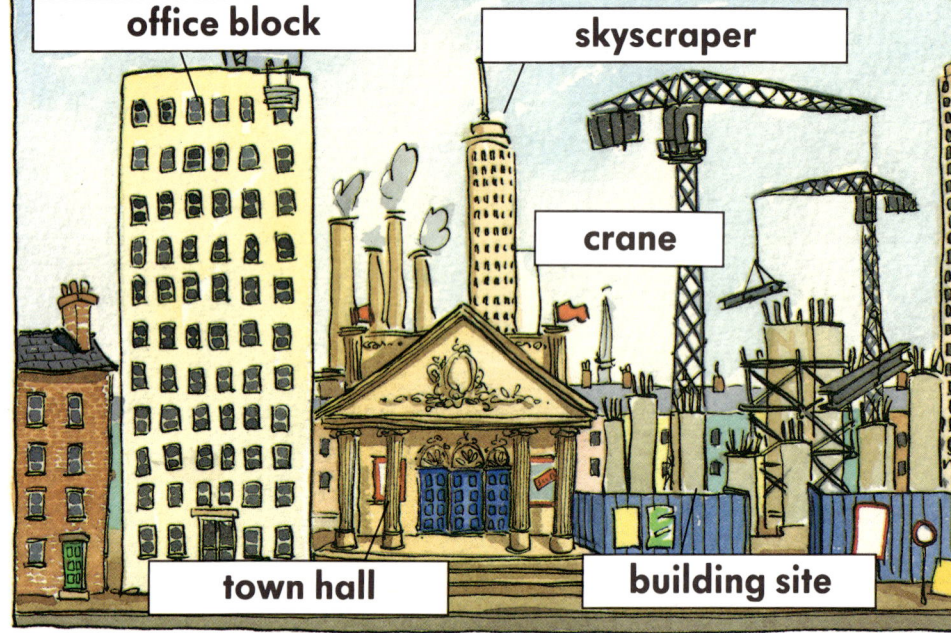

bollard A bollard is a thick post. Sometimes bollards are put in the middle of a busy road, so you have somewhere to stand when you cross.

cathedral A cathedral is a big, important church. A city usually has a cathedral.

cement mixer A cement mixer is a machine for mixing cement with sand and water. It has a big drum which turns round and round.

office block An office block is a large building with lots of offices where people work.

parking meter A parking meter is a post beside a parking space in the road. You put money in a slot when you want to park in the space.

pedestrian A pedestrian is someone who is walking along the street.

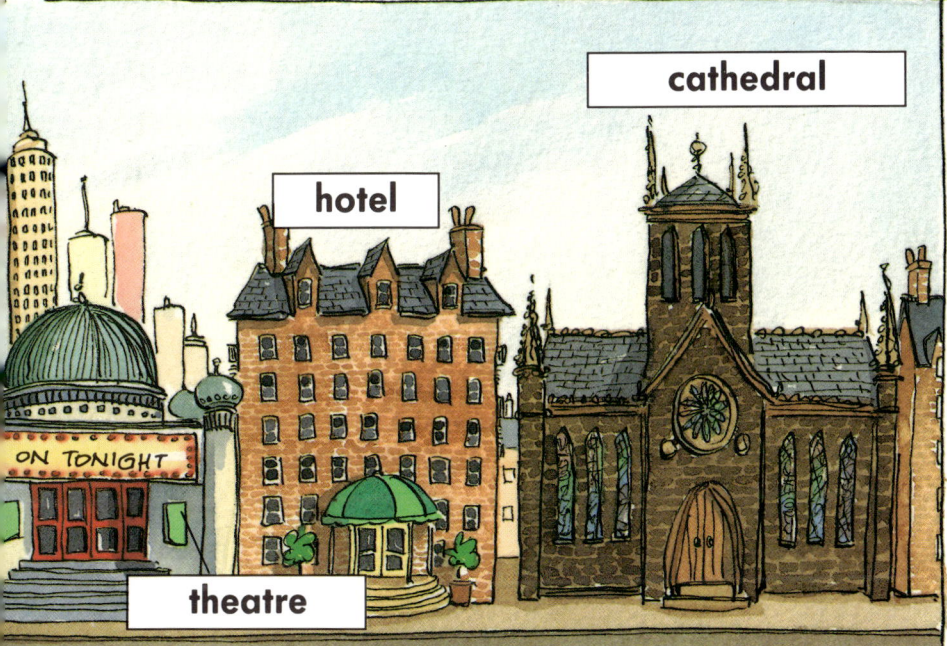

scaffolding Builders put up scaffolding to stand on when they are building or repairing high walls. It is made of metal poles and planks of wood.

skyscraper A skyscraper is a building so tall that it seems to touch the sky.

subway A subway is a tunnel under the road. You walk through it to get from one side of the road to the other.

theatre A theatre is a building with a stage and lots of seats inside. People go there to watch actors and actresses perform.

town hall The town hall is a large and grand building. The people who run a town or city work there.

traffic warden A traffic warden makes sure that cars are parked in the right place and don't block the road.

On the farm

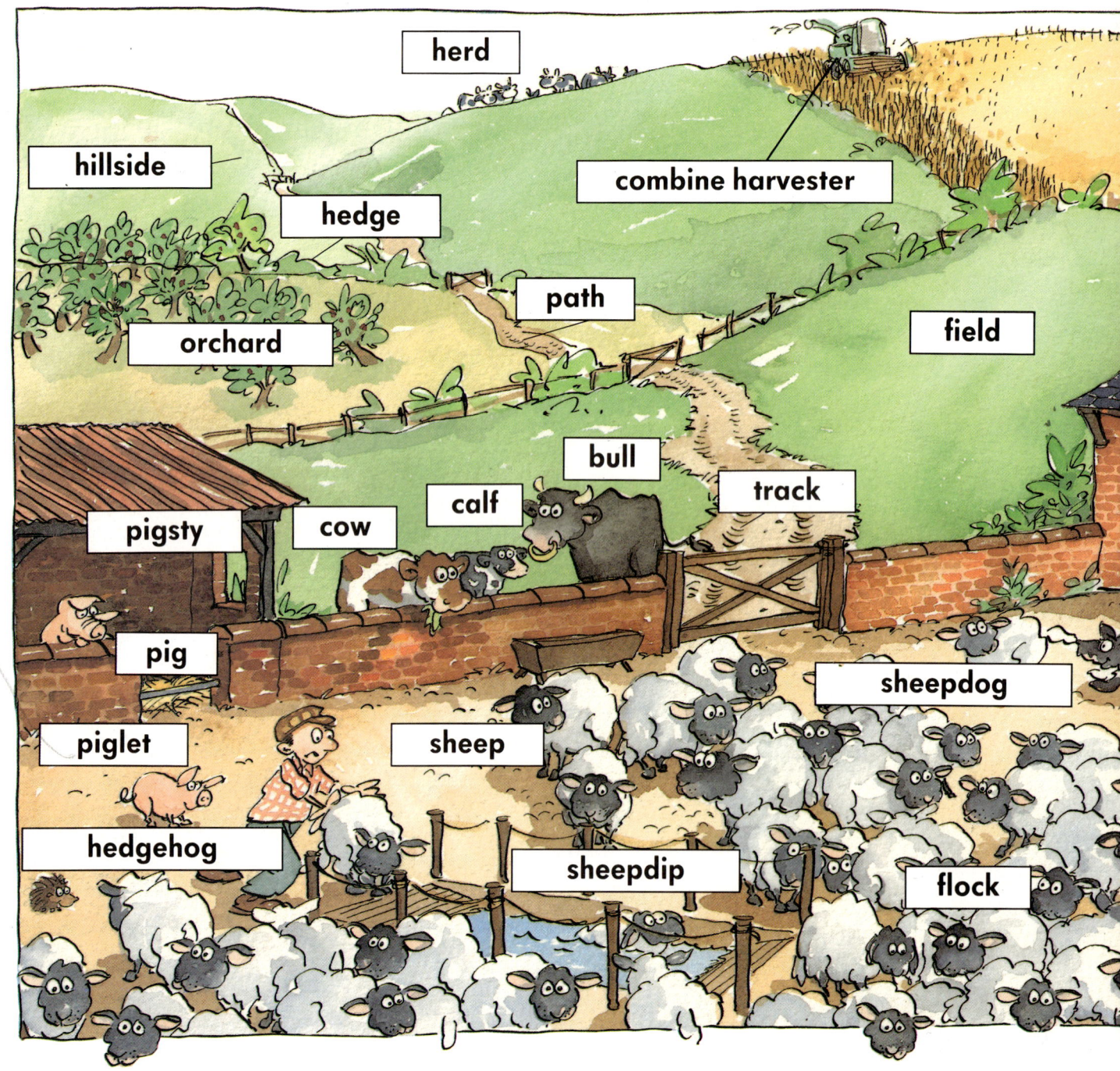

barn A barn is a big farm building where crops or animals can be kept.

combine harvester A combine harvester is a large machine. It cuts crops and sorts the grain from the stalks.

crops The plants a farmer grows are called crops.

flock A big group of sheep is called a flock.

furrow A furrow is a long, thin line in the soil where the farmer plants seeds.

hay Hay is grass that has been dried. It is used to feed animals in winter.

herd A herd is a big group of cows.

orchard An orchard is a field where lots of fruit trees grow.

pigsty A pigsty is a building where pigs live.

plough A plough is a large tool pulled by a tractor. It has sharp blades that turn the soil over.

sheepdip Farmers use a sheepdip to kill any insects in the sheep's wool.

sheepdog A sheepdog is trained to look after sheep and help the farmer move them from one field to another.

stable A stable is a building where horses are kept.

At the seaside

dinghy Dinghy is another word for a small boat.

harbour A harbour is a sheltered part of the sea where boats can be left safely.

lifebelt A lifebelt is used to keep people afloat if they fall into the water.

lifeboat A lifeboat goes out to rescue people who are in danger at sea.

lifeguard A lifeguard keeps watch and rescues people from the water if they are in danger.

lighthouse A lighthouse is a tower with a bright flashing light. The light lets ships know they are near to land or dangerous rocks.

moat A moat is a ditch filled with water around a castle.

parasol A parasol is like an umbrella, but it shades you from the sun.

snorkel A snorkel is a rubber tube you can breathe through when you are swimming underwater.

tide The tide is when the sea moves, covering and uncovering the sand.

windbreak A windbreak is made of strong material and is used to shelter you from the wind.

yacht A yacht is a boat with sails. The wind blows the sails and moves the boat along.

A port

bow The front part of a boat is called the bow.

buoy A buoy is like a coloured ball floating on the water. It is fastened to the sea bed by a long rope. Buoys let ships know where it is safe to sail.

cargo The things a ship carries are called its cargo.

container ship This is a special ship built to carry things that are packed in big metal or wooden boxes.

dock A dock is the place in a port where ships go to be loaded or unloaded.

ferry This is a ship which is used to carry people and cars.

horizon The horizon is the line you can see in the distance, where the sea seems to touch the sky.

hovercraft A hovercraft floats on a cushion of air and can travel over sea or land. It can carry people and cars.

porthole A porthole is a round window in the side of a ship.

stern The back part of a boat is called the stern.

submarine A submarine is a special kind of ship that can travel underwater.

trawler A trawler is a fishing boat with very big nets. It drags the nets through the water to catch fish.

tug Tugs are small, strong boats that can pull a big ship into port.

wake The wake is the pattern of waves a ship makes.

An airport

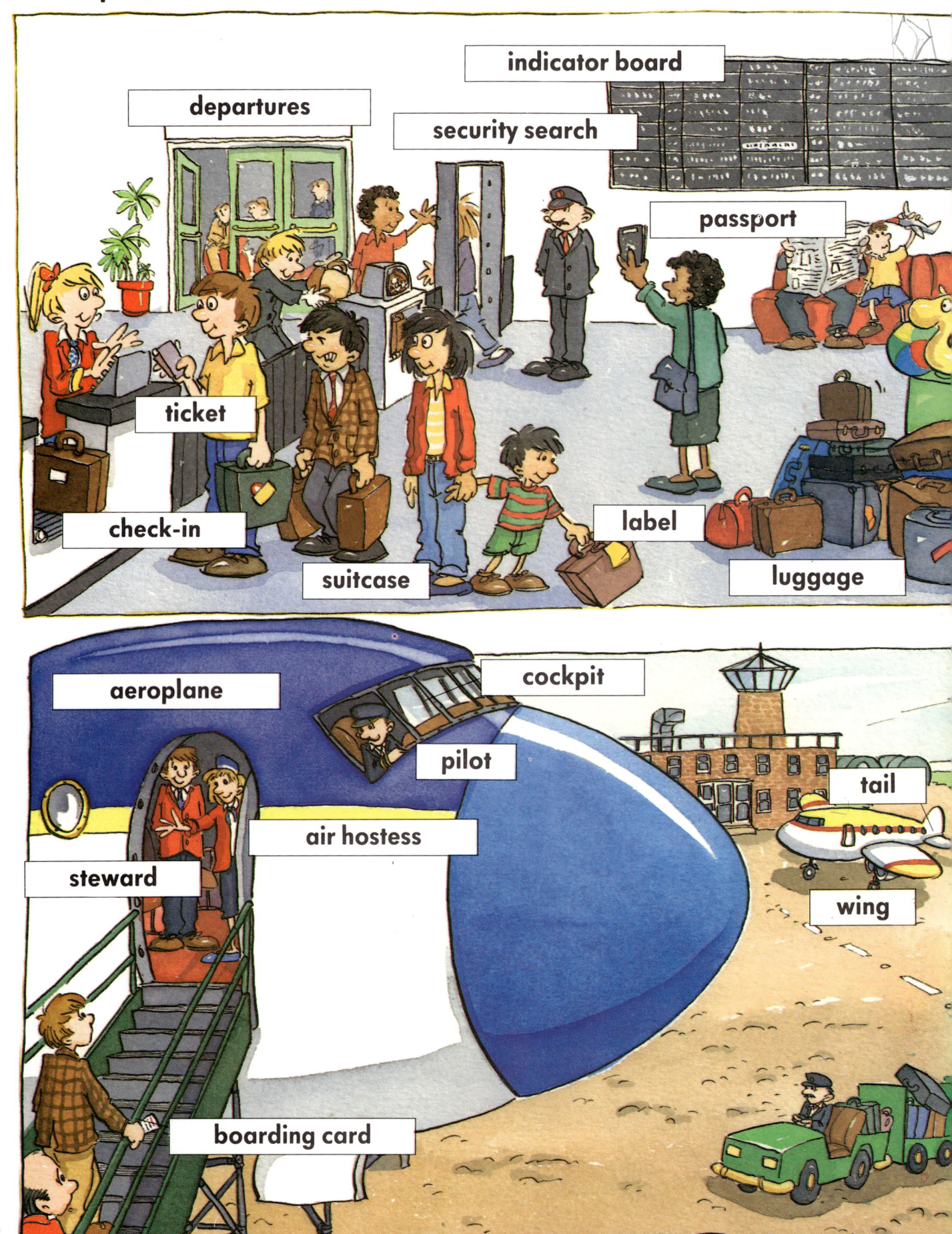

- departures
- indicator board
- security search
- passport
- ticket
- check-in
- suitcase
- label
- luggage
- aeroplane
- cockpit
- pilot
- tail
- air hostess
- steward
- wing
- boarding card

air hostess An air hostess looks after passengers on the aeroplane.

arrivals You go to this part of the airport when you are meeting someone.

baggage reclaim This is where you collect your suitcases when they come off the aeroplane.

boarding card You are given a boarding card when you show your ticket. It lets you on to the aeroplane.

check-in This is where you show your ticket and take your suitcases so they can be put on the aeroplane.

cockpit The controls of the plane are in the cockpit. The pilot sits there to fly the plane.

departures You wait in this part of the airport just before you get on the aeroplane.

hangar A hangar is like a huge garage where aeroplanes are kept.

indicator board The indicator board shows the times that planes are arriving or leaving.

luggage This is another word for your suitcases and bags.

passport A passport is a small book with your name and picture inside. You use it when you go to a different country.

security search At the security search special cameras check your bags to make sure there is nothing dangerous inside them.

steward A steward is a man who looks after the passengers on the plane.

37

At the station

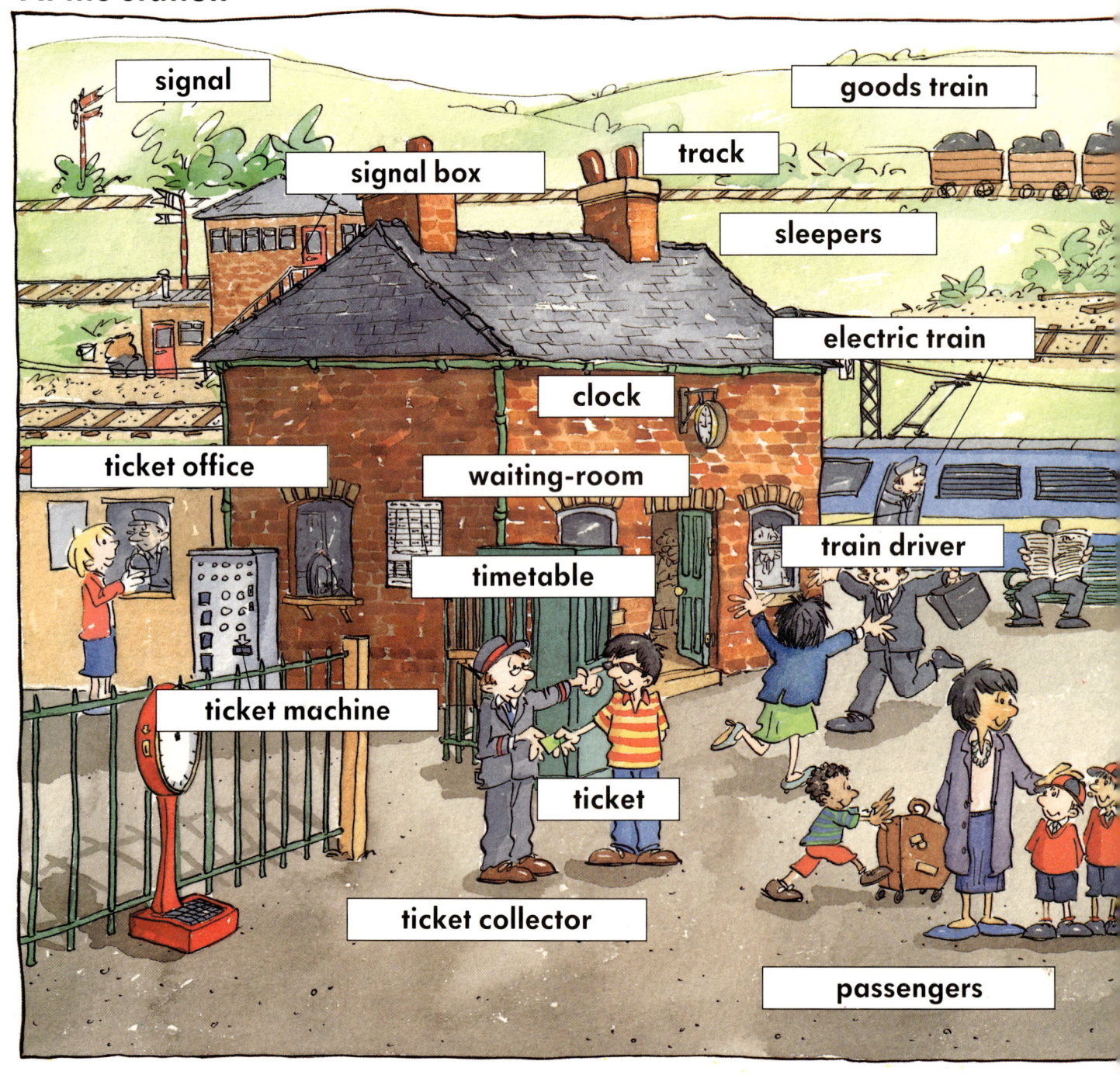

Labels in illustration: signal, goods train, signal box, track, sleepers, electric train, clock, ticket office, waiting-room, train driver, timetable, ticket machine, ticket, ticket collector, passengers

buffers Buffers are big metal springs on the end of each carriage. They protect it if the train bumps into something at the end of the track.

buffet car This is the carriage on the train where you can buy food.

diesel train A diesel train uses diesel oil in its engine to make it go.

electric train An electric train runs on electricity from wires overhead or from a rail on the ground.

goods train A goods train carries things rather than passengers.

guard The guard travels on the train and makes sure the doors are closed before the train leaves.

[Illustration labels: diesel train, engine, sleeper, luggage rack, buffet car, carriage, guard's van, buffers, guard, snack bar, porter, platform]

guard's van The guard's van has no seats. You can put bicycles or large pieces of luggage in it.

porter A porter helps people carry their luggage on and off the train.

signal box The signal box is a building beside the track. Inside there are switches to control the signals.

sleeper A sleeper is a train with beds, so people can travel overnight.

sleepers The thick planks of wood or concrete that the track lies on are called sleepers.

timetable A timetable is a list of the times when trains will arrive and leave.

In the car

car
drive
steer
accelerate
lay-by
bridge
road
bonnet
boot
indicator
headlights
tyre
number plate
bumper
roundabout
motorway
lane
breakdown
hard shoulder

accelerate When you accelerate, you make the car go faster.

brake When you brake you make the car slow down or stop.

gear lever This is a stick used to change the gears. When a car goes at different speeds it needs to use different gears.

handbrake You use the handbrake to stop the car moving when it is parked.

hard shoulder The hard shoulder is the strip of road at the side of a motorway. You can stop there if your car breaks down.

ignition key The ignition key starts the car's engine.

40

| brake | overtake | reverse |

windscreen
windscreen wiper
speedometer
steering wheel
ignition key
horn
gear lever
safety belt
handbrake

signpost
turn
park

motorway services
petrol
oil
mirror
speed limit

indicator This is a flashing orange light. It warns that the car is going to turn left or right.

lane Wide roads like motorways have two or three lanes so cars can travel side by side. The lanes are marked with white lines.

reverse When you reverse, you make the car go backwards.

speed limit The speed limit on a road shows how fast you are allowed to go.

speedometer The speedometer shows how fast the car is going.

Space and space travel

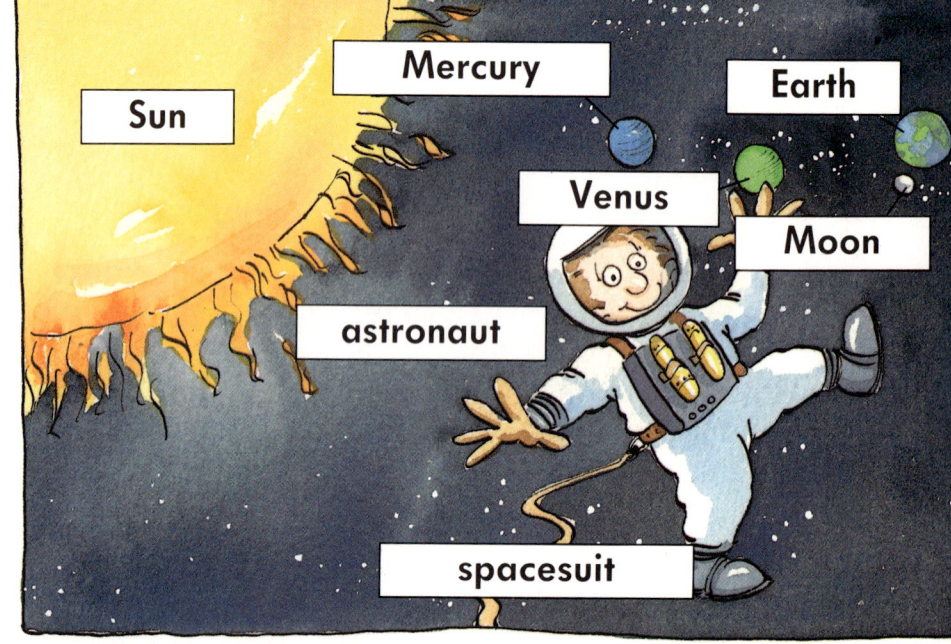

telescope

galaxy

star

mission control

Sun · Mercury · Venus · Earth · Moon · astronaut · spacesuit

rocket

lift off

shuttle

satellite

comet Comets travel round the sun leaving a bright trail behind them.

crater A crater is a hole in the surface of a planet.

galaxy A galaxy is an enormous group of stars and planets.

meteorite A meteorite is rock from space that falls to Earth.

moon A moon is a small planet. Moons travel around other planets. Our Moon goes around the Earth every four weeks.

mission control Mission control is the place where people control a spacecraft from the ground.

planet — comet — meteorite

Mars — Jupiter — spacecraft — Uranus — Saturn — Neptune — Pluto — parachute — space — touchdown

space station — crater — moon buggy

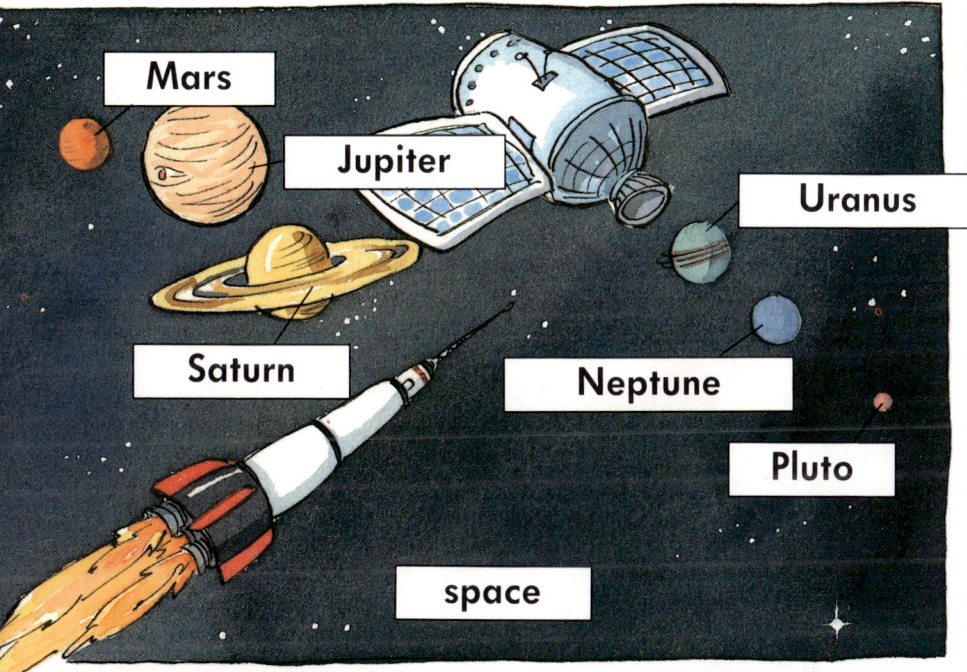

planet A planet is like a huge round ball in space. Planets travel around stars. The Earth is a planet and the star it travels around is the Sun.

satellite A satellite is a spacecraft that travels round and round a planet. Satellites are used to send messages or collect information.

shuttle A space shuttle is a spacecraft that can be used lots of times.

space station A space station is a large spacecraft where astronauts can stay in space.

star A star is a like a huge ball of fire in space. The sun is a star. Most stars look like tiny lights in the sky because they are a long way from Earth.

Machines we use

Labels in illustration: television, screen, portable, video recorder, camera, telephone, calculator, remote control, answering machine, computer, print-out, printer, disk, instructions, keyboard

aerial An aerial picks up signals for television and radio programmes.

answering machine You connect an answering machine to a telephone. It records messages from people who phone when you are out.

disk Instructions and information for computers are stored on disks.

fast forward This button makes the tape recorder wind forwards quickly.

instructions The instructions tell you how to use a machine properly.

portable A portable television is small enough to be carried from one room to another.

Labels in illustration: aerial, radio, tapes, videos, volume control, records, record player, turntable, speakers, cassette recorder, headphones, fast forward, rewind, record, play, cable

print-out The paper that comes from a computer's printer is called the print-out.

record You use this button to record a programme or music on tape so it can be heard or seen again.

remote control The remote control lets you use a machine from a short distance away.

rewind This button makes the tape wind back to the beginning.

turntable This is the flat part of the record player where you put the record.

volume control The volume control knob is used to make the sound louder or quieter.

45

Measuring things

size
medium-sized
small
big
huge
wide
tiny
height
weight
kilograms
scales
span
stride

1 **2**

centimetres Centimetres are used to measure how long or how high something is. A table could be measured in centimetres.

grams Grams are used to measure weight. The weight of one apple or some sweets would be measured in grams.

kilograms Kilograms are also used to measure weight. The weight of a person or a sack of potatoes would be measured in kilograms.

litres Litres are used to measure liquid. Water or milk can be measured in litres.

shapes

circle • oval • triangle • star • crescent • diamond • square • rectangle

long • short • thin

grams • measuring jug • cup • spoon • litres • tape measure • centimetres • metres • ruler

3 4

measuring jug This is a jug with measurements marked on the side. It is used for measuring liquids.

metres Metres are used to measure how long or how high something is. A room could be measured in metres.

scales Scales are used to weigh things in grams and kilograms.

span A span is the distance from the tip of your thumb to your little finger.

stride A stride is a long step. In the past, people would measure their land in strides.

47

Words for stories

abracadabra This is a word you say when you want some magic to happen.

adventure An adventure is something you do that is unusual, exciting or dangerous.

cauldron A cauldron is a big, metal cooking pot. Witches use them for making magic potions.

dinosaur Dinosaurs are huge animals that lived millions of years ago.

drawbridge This is a special kind of bridge. It can be pulled up to stop people crossing.

gangplank Pirates made their prisoners walk along the gang-plank until they fell into the sea.

highwayman A highwayman was a robber who rode on horseback. He stopped travellers and stole from them.

pirate A pirate was a robber who sailed the seas and stole from other ships.

skull and crossbones This picture was on the flag of pirate ships. It meant that death and danger were nearby.

spell When you cast a spell you do some magic. Witches, wizards and fairies cast spells.

unicorn A unicorn is a storybook animal. It looks like a white horse with a horn growing from its forehead.

wizard A wizard is a man who can do magical things.

adventure

abracadabra

cauldron

broomstick

magic carpet

wand

unicorn

magic

wizard

spell

witch

dinosaur

pistol

giant

highwayman

dagger

cloak

fairy

pixie

toadstool

49

Time

calendar

day	
Monday	tea at Grandma's
Tuesday	horse riding
Wednesday	swimming lesson
Thursday	dentist
Friday	Lucy's house
Saturday	School fete
Sunday	Sam's party

eight o'clock   **half past two**

quarter to seven   **quarter past eleven**

morning

clock
minute
hour

afternoon

evening

night

seasons

spring

month

March

April

May

summer

June

July

August

autumn

September

October

November

winter

December

January

February

51

Colours and numbers

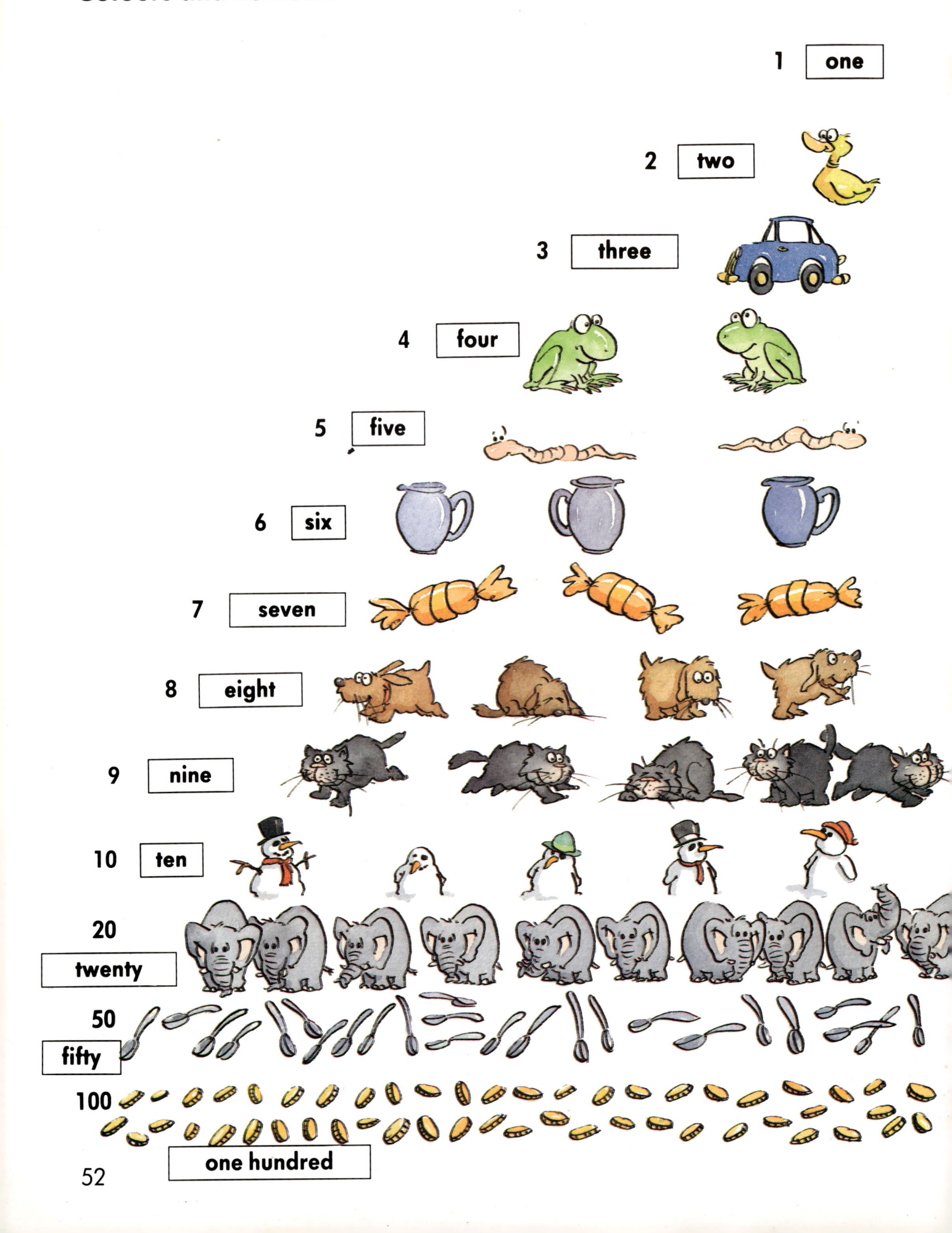

1 one
2 two
3 three
4 four
5 five
6 six
7 seven
8 eight
9 nine
10 ten
20 twenty
50 fifty
100 one hundred

52

Millions

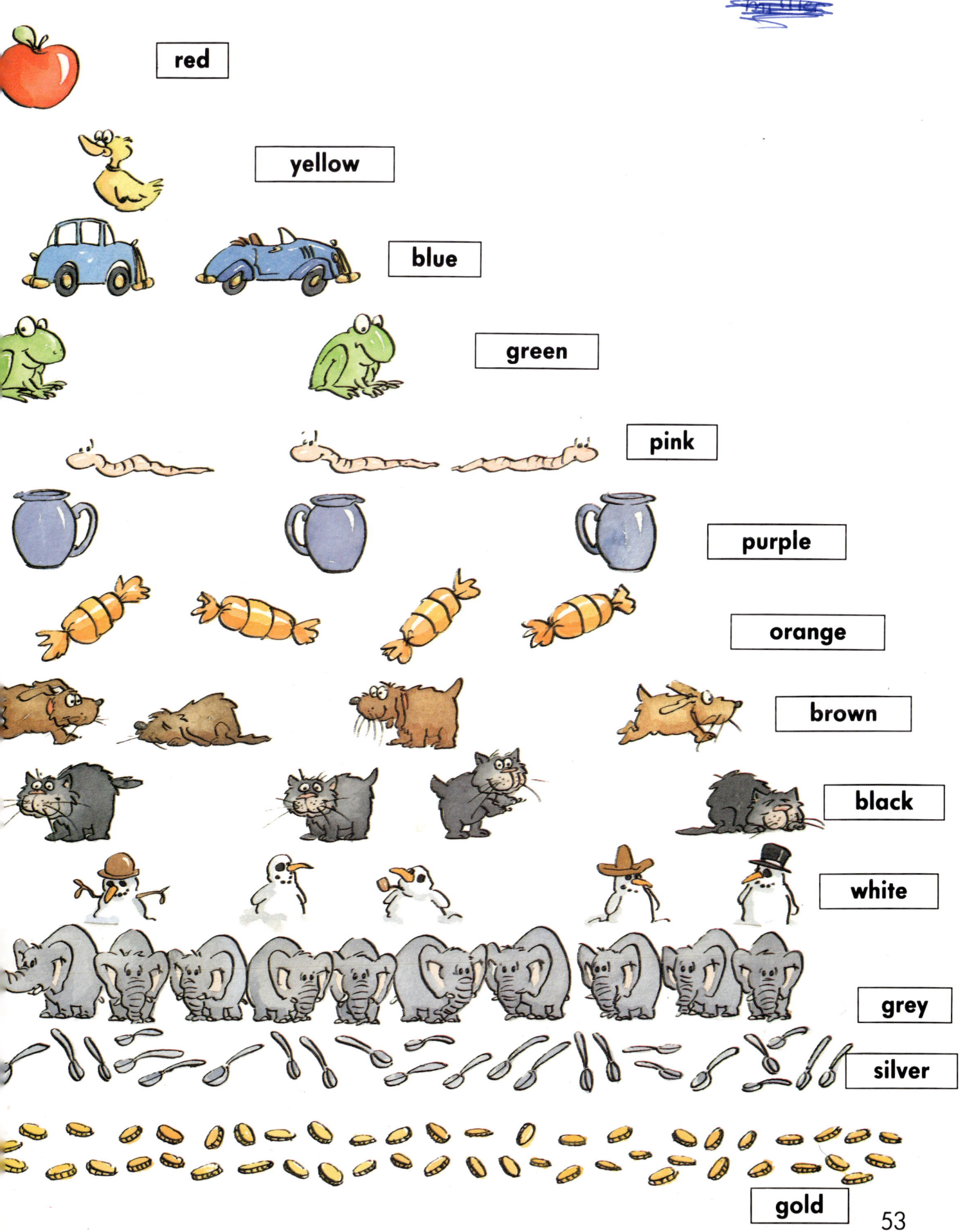

red

yellow

blue

green

pink

purple

orange

brown

black

white

grey

silver

gold

53

Opposites

slow	fast
long	short	light	heavy
large	small	sharp	blunt
hot	cold
angry	calm
awake	asleep	full	empty
solid	liquid	fat	thin
old	new
dry	wet
same	different	open	closed
shiny	dull

happy	sad	straight	curved
dark / light	left / right	soft	hard
clean	dirty	forwards / backwards	noisy / quiet
dead / alive	hard / easy	slack	tight
strong	weak	back	bitter
smooth	rough	front	sweet

Action words

talk listen carry perform fall

touch show watch point stand sit

explore run walk crawl

knit sew relax make paint

drop give take exercise stretch

ride pull push stick

lose find jump build whisper

dance cut shout break mend

57

Position words

last
third
second
first
above
on
over
below
inside
outside
under
against
up
behind
in front of
beside
between
down

Words in this book

above, 58
abracadabra, 48
accelerate, 40
accountant, 26
acorn, 20
actor, 27
actress, 27
adult, 4
adventure, 48
aerial, 44
aeroplane, 36
afternoon, 50
against, 58
air hostess, 37
aisle, 16
alive, 55
alphabet, 14
ambulance, 25
anaesthetic, 24
anchor, 34
angry, 54
ankle, 6
answering machine, 44
April, 51
architect, 26
arm, 6
arrivals, 37
asleep, 54
assistant, 16
astronaut, 27, 42
athletics, 22
August, 51
auntie, 4
autumn, 51
aviary, 20
awake, 54

back, 55
back door, 8
backwards, 55
bacon, 17
badger, 31
baggage reclaim, 37
baker, 16
ball, 20
bandage, 25
banker, 27
bargain, 16
barn, 30
baseball, 22
basket ball, 23
bathroom, 8

beach, 33
beans, 16
bedroom, 8
bee, 13
behind, 58
below, 58
berries, 13
beside, 58
between, 58
bicycle, 20
big, 46
biscuits, 17
bitter, 55
black, 53
blackboard, 15
blood, 7
blue, 53
blunt, 54
boarding card, 37
boiler, 9
bollard, 28
bones, 7
bonnet, 40
books, 15
boot, 40
bounce, 20
bow, 35
bowl, 10
boxing, 22
brain, 7
brake, 40
bread, 16
break, 57
breakdown, 40
bricks, 8
bridge, 40
broomstick, 49
brother, 4
brown, 53
brush, 11
bucket, 11, 32
bud, 13
buffers, 38
buffet car, 38
build, 57
builder, 8
building site, 28
bulb, 13
bull, 30
bumper, 40
buoy, 35
bus stop, 28

bush, 13
butcher, 16
butter, 16
butterfly, 12

cable, 45
café, 18
cake, 18
calculator, 44
calendar, 50
calf, 6, 30
calm, 54
camera, 44
captain, 34
car, 28, 40
car park, 29
cargo, 35
carriage, 39
carry, 56
cassette recorder, 45
castle, 48
catch, 20
cathedral, 28
cauldron, 48
ceiling, 8
cement mixer, 28
centimetres, 46
cereal, 16
chalk, 15
chart, 25
chase, 21
check-in, 37
check-up, 24
checkout, 16
cheese, 16
chef, 19
cheque, 16
chest, 6
chicken, 31
child, 5
children, 21
chimney, 8
chin, 6
chips, 18
circle, 47
classroom, 14
clean, 55
cleaner, 26
cliff, 33
climbing frame, 20
cloak, 49
clock, 38, 50

59

closed, 54
clothes, 17
club, 22
cobbler, 17
cockerel, 31
cockpit, 37
coffee, 17, 18
cold, 54
collage, 14
colours, 52
combine harvester, 30
comet, 42
compost, 13
computer, 44
computer programmer, 26
concentrate, 14
conker, 20
container ship, 35
conveyor belt, 17
cooker, 10
counter, 19
court, 22
cousin, 4
cow, 30
crab, 33
crane, 28
crater, 42
crawl, 56
crayons, 14
credit card, 17
crescent, 47
cricket, 22
crockery, 10
crops, 30
crowd, 28
crutches, 25
cup, 47
cupboard, 10
curved, 55
customer, 16
cut, 57
cutlery, 19
cymbals, 14

dagger, 49
dance, 57
dancer, 26
dark, 55
day, 50
daydream, 14
dead, 55
December, 51
deciduous, 20

dentist, 24
department store, 17
departures, 37
designer, 27
dessert, 19
diamond, 47
diesel train, 38
different, 54
digger, 29
dinghy, 32
dinosaur, 48
dirty, 55
dishwasher, 10
disk, 44
diving, 23
D.I.Y., 9
dock, 35
doctor, 24
down, 58
dragon, 48
draining board, 10
drainpipe, 9
drawbridge, 48
drawer, 10
dream, 48
drill, 12
drive, 40
drop, 57
drum, 14
dry, 54
dry cleaner, 17
duckpond, 20
dull, 54
dustman, 27

ears, 7
Earth, 42
easel, 14
easy, 55
eight, 52
elbow, 6
electric cable, 9
electric train, 38
electrician, 9
empty, 54
engine, 39
engineer, 26
evening, 50
evergreen, 20
exercise, 57
explore, 56
eyes, 7

fairy, 49
fall, 56
family, 4
farmhouse, 31
farmyard, 31
fast, 54
fast forward, 44
fat, 54
father, 4
February, 51
ferry, 35
fidget, 14
field, 30
fifty, 52
find, 57
fireman, 26
fireplace, 8
first, 58
fish, 34
five, 52
flock, 30
floor, 8
florist, 17
flour, 16
flowerbed, 13
flowers, 17
food mixer, 10
foot, 6
fork, 12
forwards, 55
foundations, 9
fountain, 28
four, 52
freezer, 10
Friday, 50
fridge, 11
friend, 4
front, 55
front door, 9
fruit, 16
fruit juice, 18
frying pan, 10
full, 54
funnel, 34
furniture, 16
furrow, 30

galaxy, 42
gangplank, 48
gardener, 27
gas pipe, 8
gear lever, 40
germinate, 13

giant, 49
give, 57
globe, 15
glue, 14
goal, 22
goalkeeper, 22
goat, 31
gold, 53
golf, 22
goods train, 38
grams, 46
grandparents, 4
green, 53
greengrocer, 16
greenhouse, 13
grey, 53
grill, 10
grocer, 16
groceries, 16
guard, 38
guard's van, 39
gutter, 9
gymnastics, 22

hair, 7
hairdresser, 26
hamburger, 18
hammer, 12
hand, 6
handbrake, 40
handstand, 20
hangar, 37
happy, 55
harbour, 32
harbour wall, 32
hard, 55
hard shoulder, 40
hay, 30
head, 6
headlights, 40
headphones, 45
heart, 7
heavy, 54
hedge, 30
hedgehog, 30
height, 46
herd, 30
hide-and-seek, 21
high chair, 19
highwayman, 48
hillside, 30
hip, 6
horizon, 35

horn, 41
horse, 31
horse racing, 23
hosepipe, 12
hospital, 25
hot, 54
hotel, 29
hour, 50
hovercraft, 35
huge, 46
husband, 5

ice-cream, 17, 18
ice-skating, 23
ignition key, 40
in front of, 58
indicator, 41
indicator board, 37
ingredients, 10
injection, 25
inside, 58
instructions, 44
intestine, 7

jam, 17
jam jar, 15
January, 51
jellyfish, 32
jockey, 22
joiner, 9
journalist, 26
judge, 27
judo, 22
July, 51
jump, 57
June, 51
Jupiter, 43

keyboard, 44
kilograms, 46
kitchen, 8
knee, 6
knife, 10
knit, 56

label, 36
lamp-post, 28
lane, 41
large, 54
last, 58
lawn, 13
lawnmower, 12
lay-by, 40

left, 55
leg, 6
letter, 17
lifebelt, 32
lifeboat, 32
lifeguard, 32
lift, 16
lift off, 42
light, 54, 55
lighthouse, 32
limpet, 32
liquid, 54
listen, 56
litres, 46
litter bin, 21
liver, 7
living room, 8
lobster, 34
loft, 9
long, 47, 54
lorry driver, 26
lose, 57
luggage, 37
luggage rack, 39
lungs, 7

magic, 49
magic carpet, 49
magnifying glass, 15
main course, 19
make, 56
March, 51
Mars, 43
mask, 24
May, 51
meal, 18
measure, 15
measuring jug, 47
meat, 16
mechanic, 27
medium-sized, 46
mend, 57
menu, 18
Mercury, 42
meteorite, 42
metres, 47
microwave, 11
milk, 16, 18
miner, 26
minute, 50
mirror, 41
mission control, 42
moat, 33

model, 15, 27
Monday, 50
month, 51
moon, 42
moon buggy, 43
mop, 11
morning, 50
moss, 13
mother, 5
motor racing, 23
motorway, 40
motorway services, 41
mouth, 7
muscles, 7
music, 14
musician, 27

nails, 12
neck, 6
neighbours, 5
Neptune, 43
new, 54
newsagent, 16
newspapers, 16
night, 50
nine, 52
noisy, 55
nose, 6
November, 51
number plate, 40
numbers, 15, 52
nurse, 25

ocean, 34
October, 51
octopus, 34
office block, 28
oil, 41
old, 54
on, 58
one, 52
one hundred, 52
open, 54
operating theatre, 24
operation, 24
opposites, 54
orange, 53
orange juice, 16
orchard, 31
outside, 58
oval, 47
oven, 10
over, 58

overtake, 41

paint, 14, 56
painter, 26
parachute, 43
parasol, 33
parents, 5
park, 41
park-keeper, 21
parking meter, 28
parrot, 48
passengers, 38
passport, 37
path, 30
patient, 24
pavement, 28
pebble, 33
pedestrian, 28
pencil, 15
pepper, 19
perform, 56
petrol, 41
pet, 5
photographer, 26
picnic, 21
pig, 30
piglet, 30
pigsty, 31
pilot, 36
pink, 53
pirate, 48
pistol, 49
pitch, 23
pixie, 59
pizza, 17, 18
planet, 43
plants, 13
plaster, 25
plasterer, 9
plates, 11
platform, 39
play, 20, 45
plough, 31
plug, 11
plumber, 9
Pluto, 43
point, 56
politician, 27
portable, 44
porter, 25, 39
porthole, 35
post office, 17
postman, 26

power boat, 33
prawns, 34
prescription, 24
price, 16
print-out, 45
printer, 44
pull, 57
pupil, 14
purple, 53
push, 57

queue, 28
quiet, 55

rabbit, 31
racquet, 23
radiator, 9
radio, 45
read, 15
receipt, 17
receptionist, 24
recipe, 11
record, 45
record player, 45
recorder, 14
records, 45
rectangle, 47
red, 53
reeds, 21
referee, 23
register, 15
relative, 5
relax, 56
remote control, 45
restaurant, 19
reverse, 41
rewind, 45
ribs, 7
ride, 57
right, 55
road, 29, 40
rock pool, 32
rocket, 42
roller-skates, 21
rolling pin, 10
roof, 8
roots, 13
rough, 55
roundabout, 40
ruler, 47
run, 56
runway, 37

62

sad, 55
safety belt, 41
safety helmet, 29
sailing, 23
sailor, 27, 35
salad, 18
sale, 17
salesperson, 27
salt, 19
same, 54
sand, 33
sand castle, 33
sandwich, 18
satellite, 43
Saturday, 50
Saturn, 43
saucepan, 10
sausage, 18
savoury, 19
saw, 12
scaffolding, 29
scales, 15, 47
scientist, 27
scissors, 14
score, 23
screen, 44
sea, 33
seagull, 34
seasons, 51
seaweed, 33
second, 58
secretary, 27
security search, 37
seeds, 13
seesaw, 20
self-service, 19
September, 51
serviette, 18
seven, 52
sew, 56
shapes, 47
sharp, 54
shears, 12
shed, 12
sheep, 30
sheepdip, 31
sheepdog, 31
shell, 32
shiny, 54
shoes, 17
shoots, 12
shopping centre, 28
short, 47, 54

shoulder, 6
shout, 57
show, 56
shuttle, 43
sieve, 11
signal, 38
signal box, 39
signpost, 41
silver, 53
singer, 27
sink, 10
siren, 29
sister, 5
sit, 56
six, 52
size, 46
skeleton, 6
skiing, 23
skipping rope, 20
skull, 7
skull and crossbones, 48
skyscraper, 29
slack, 55
sleeper, 39
sleepers, 39
slide, 21
slow, 54
small, 46, 54
small fork, 13
smooth, 55
snack, 19
snack bar, 39
snail, 12
snorkel, 33
soccer, 22
soft, 55
soldier, 26
solid, 54
somersault, 21
space, 43
spacecraft, 43
space station, 43
spacesuit, 42
spade, 12, 32
spaghetti, 18
span, 47
spatula, 11
speakers, 45
speed limit, 41
speedometer, 41
spell, 48
spoon, 47
spread, 17

spring, 51
sprinkler, 13
square, 47
squash, 23
squirrel, 20
stable, 31
staircase, 9
stand, 56
star, 43, 47
starfish, 32
starter, 19
statue, 21
steam, 11
steer, 40
steering wheel, 41
stepladder, 12
stern, 35
stethoscope, 25
steward, 37
stick, 57
stitches, 25
stomach, 7
straight, 55
street, 28
stretch, 57
stretcher, 25
stride, 47
strong, 55
submarine, 35
subway, 29
sugar, 16
suitcase, 36
summer, 51
sun, 42
sunbathe, 32
Sunday, 50
supermarket, 17
surgeon, 25
surgery, 25
surname, 5
swan, 20
sweet, 55
swimming, 23
swimsuit, 33
syringe, 25

table, 10
tail, 36
take, 57
talk, 56
tape measure, 47
tapes, 45
taps, 10

63

taxi driver, 26
tea, 18
teacher, 14
teenager, 5
telephone, 44
telescope, 42
television, 44
ten, 52
tennis, 23
theatre, 29
thermometer, 25
thigh, 6
thin, 47, 54
think, 15
third, 58
three, 52
throw, 20
Thursday, 50
ticket, 36, 38
ticket collector, 38
ticket machine, 38
ticket office, 38
tide, 33
tight, 55
tiles, 9
till, 17
time, 50
timer, 11
timetable, 39
tiny, 46
toadstool, 49
toilet, 8
toilet roll, 17
touch, 56
touchdown, 43
towel, 32
town hall, 29
toy shop, 17
toys, 17
track, 30, 38
tractor, 31
traffic jam, 29
traffic lights, 28
traffic warden, 29
trailer, 31
train driver, 38
trawler, 35
tray, 18
trays, 14
treasure, 48
triangle, 14, 47
trolley, 17, 19, 25, 37
trowel, 13

64

truck, 28
Tuesday, 50
tug, 35
turn, 41
turntable, 45
TV presenter, 26
twenty, 52
twins, 5
two, 52
tyre, 40

umpire, 23
uncle, 5
under, 58
unicorn, 48
uniform, 25
up, 58
Uranus, 43

vegetables, 16
veins, 7
Venus, 42
vet, 27
video recorder, 44
videos, 45
village, 31
volume control, 45

waiter, 19
waitress, 19
waiting-room, 24, 38
wake, 35
walk, 56
wand, 49
ward, 25
washing, 11
washing machine, 11
washing powder, 17
washing-up liquid, 17
watch, 56
water pipes, 8
water-ski, 33
water tank, 9
waves, 33
weak, 55
weather forecaster, 26
Wednesday, 50
weed, 13
weigh, 15
weight, 46
wet, 54
wheelbarrow, 12
wheelchair, 25

whisper, 57
white, 53
wide, 46
wife, 5
windbreak, 33
window cleaner, 26
windscreen, 41
windscreen wiper, 41
windsurf, 32
wing, 36
winter, 51
witch, 49
wizard, 48
wood, 31
worm, 12
wrist, 6
write, 15

yacht, 33
yellow, 53
yoghurt, 17, 18

zebra crossing, 28